A POETIC PRIMER FOR LOVE AND SEDUCTION: NASO WAS MY TUTOR

Other Emma Press anthologies:

The Emma Press Anthology of Mildly Erotic Verse
The Emma Press Anthology of Motherhood (Feb 2014)
The Emma Press Anthology of Fatherhood (May 2014)

The Emma Press Picks:

The Flower and the Plough, by Rachel Piercey
The Emmores, by Richard O'Brien
The Held and the Lost, by Kristen Roberts (Feb 2014)
Captain Love and the Five Joaquins, by John Clegg (May 2014)

Pamphlets:

Raspberries for the Ferry, by Andrew Wynn Owen (Mar 2014)
Ikhda, by Ikhda, by Ikhda Ayuning Maharsi (Mar 2014)

A Poetic Primer for
LOVE AND SEDUCTION:
Naso was my Tutor

EDITED BY RACHEL PIERCEY AND EMMA WRIGHT

with poems from Jo Brandon, John Canfield, Jade Cuttle,
Amy Key, Anja Konig, Cheryl Moskowitz, Abigail Parry,
Rachel Piercey, Richard O'Brien, Christopher Reid,
Jacqueline Saphra, Liane Strauss, Nicola Warwick,
Ruth Wiggins and Andrew Wynn Owen

THE EMMA PRESS

THE EMMA PRESS

First published in Great Britain in 2014
by the Emma Press Ltd

Poems copyright © individual copyright holders 2014
Selection copyright © Rachel Piercey and Emma Wright 2014
Illustrations and introduction copyright © Emma Wright 2014

All rights reserved.

The right of Rachel Piercey and Emma Wright to be identified
as the editors of this work has been asserted by them in accordance
with the Copyright, Designs and Patents Act 1988.

ISBN 978-0-9574596-3-2

A CIP catalogue record of this book
is available from the British Library.

Printed and bound in Great Britain
by Volume Ltd, Reading.

theemmapress.com
editor@theemmapress.com

Fig. I. Erogenous Zones

CONTENTS

PREFACE ix

THE ART OF LOVE

Seduction — RUTH WIGGINS	1
The Theory of Fireworks — ANJA KONIG	4
The Connoisseur — CHRISTOPHER REID	6
The Giveaway — NICOLA WARWICK	9
Advice to Members of the Uniformed Professions — RICHARD O'BRIEN	10
Myrtus — RUTH WIGGINS	12
How To Be Sexy — AMY KEY	14
Take your Positions — ANDREW WYNN OWEN	16
The Lesson from the Snake — ABIGAIL PARRY	18
Forget what you've been told — JO BRANDON	20
Dear body — JADE CUTTLE	23
Spring Fever Summer Cold — ANJA KONIG	24
I Give You This as a Token — CHERYL MOSKOWITZ	25
Strategies for the Monogamous — JACQUELINE SAPHRA	26
Strategies for the Adulterous — JACQUELINE SAPHRA	27
How To Have An Affair — AMY KEY	28

CURES FOR LOVE

    A&E — LIANE STRAUSS   33

    Medicine — RACHEL PIERCEY   34

    52 Card Pickup — ABIGAIL PARRY   36

    Elixir Amore — JOHN CANFIELD   37

    With this ring — RACHEL PIERCEY   38

ACKNOWLEDGMENTS   41

ABOUT THE POETS   43

ABOUT THE EMMA PRESS   47

LIST OF ILLUSTRATIONS

(*all depicting suggestions taken directly from the* Ars Amatoria *and* Remedia Amoris)

FIG. I. EROGENOUS ZONES   v

FIG. II. KEY QUALITIES IN LOVERS   7

FIG. III. GIFTS FOR YOUR SWEETHEART   8

FIG. IV. HOW TO DISGUISE DEFICIENCIES   22

FIG. V. FOUR WAYS TO LOSE YOUR LOVER   32

PREFACE

Our purpose in creating this book has been to provide the average student with such knowledge and understanding as are essential to the art of love. Love may be wild and unpredictable, but as with all arts it can be mastered through diligent study and the application of technique. We have assembled in this primer a collection of poems designed to guide lovers of all abilities and backgrounds in the practices of finding and falling in love, inspired by and covering similar ground to the *Ars Amatoria* and *Remedia Amoris*, by the Roman poet Publius Ovidius Naso (Ovid), and additionally exploring areas felt by the poets to be relevant to the modern student.

In commissioning material for this book, we turned to poets rather than advice columnists or sexperts, hoping to draw on the same rich vein of considered wisdom that served us well in *The Emma Press Anthology of Mildly Erotic Verse* (2013). We invoked the spirits of Cupid and Casanova, Cypris and Cilla Black, and were fortunate enough to receive contributions from fifteen poets whose cumulative experience in the field is unparalleled.

Ruth Wiggins (*Seduction*, p. 1-3) sings of armpits and men, while Christopher Reid (*The Connoisseur*, p. 6) advises oenophiles and Amy Key runs through some hard-and-fast rules in *How To Be Sexy* (p. 14-5). Nicola Warwick (*The Giveaway*, p. 9) prepares the reader for a date and Andrew Wynn Owen has a number of suggestions for dessert (*Take your Positions*, p. 16-7); Richard O'Brien (*Advice to Members of the Uniformed Professions*, p. 10-11) makes a compelling case for keeping your hat or badge on, and Abigail Parry

(*Lesson from the Snake*, p. 18-9) suggests keeping your mouth shut too. Tentative lovers receive bracing guidance from Jo Brandon (*Forget what you've been told*, p. 20-1) and Jade Cuttle (*Dear body*, p. 23), while Anja Konig coughs up a frank account of falling in love in *Spring Fever Summer Cold* (p. 24). Cheryl Moskowitz (*I Give You This as a Token*, p. 25) and Jacqueline Saphra (*Strategies for the Monogamous*, p. 26) offer advanced suggestions for those who are in it for the long-haul.

What of the broken-hearted? Can there be advice for the leavers and the left? In the second part of the book, Liane Strauss issues comfort and compassion in *A&E* (p. 33), while Abigail Parry deals out harsh truths in *52 Card Pickup* (p. 36). Keen to succour, Rachel Piercey shares her prescription from the witchdoctor (*Medicine*, p. 34-5) as well as pointers for an exorcism (*With this ring*, p. 38-9), and John Canfield shares the keys to his liqueur cabinet (*Elixir Amore*, p. 37).

We are confident in the power of these poems to develop and enhance the natural gifts of any eager lover, and we hope that this book will become a treasured resource in many students' libraries. If this book helps even one person to take up and excel at the art of love then we shall be satisfied.

Emma Wright

WINNERSH
January, 2014

THE ART OF LOVE

Seduction

Sweet thing! Don't sigh. Take it from me.
You'll never catch him, red-eyed, tissues
up your sleeve. But I can teach you
how to make him weep.

Half the problem is the company you keep.
Those girls, those magazines.
The advice they give is all very well,
if you want nothing but the company of geese.

But they misguide you. Trust me.

*

Take Venus, she runs the circus.
Broad and gaudy, sweet mischief
at her hip, she holds court
in a simple straw and sawdust ring.

Sure, she tricks it out. A string
of busted lights, some toffee on a stick.
But what she doesn't say is – the punters
come, regardless.

There is no point pretending
you're anything you're not. You simply
have to accent what you've actually got.

And know the game is rigged.

*

2

Now I can teach you the wide-eyed tricks,
the ones to captivate, to play for keeps.

Afraid to reach for coffee on the shelf?
Worried he might catch a glimpse –
the unruly glitter of your pretty armpit?

Go on, reach.

He'll go home with a taste of the illicit.
If he goes home at all, that is.

*

Likewise, that wilful button
on your favourite shirt, when you feel it slip
pretend you haven't noticed it.

*

Give him an opportunity to stare –
forget yourself in a public space.

Lose yourself in something solitary.

A book? Sure, but better yet – try
whittling. You think I'm kidding,
but wait and see how he warms
to your way with a staff of beech.

*

It's convenient to believe in magic.
And since it's convenient, let us believe.
Believe in your ability to enchant him.

Knock up a little Pousse l'Amour.
Take your egg yolk, your maraschino.
Add brandy as a stiffener. Rhubarb, hyssop.

Spend time macerating, pounding
in a jar. Your wrist action will be
something to inspire.

Let him sip it off your spoon.

He'll be yours, a lemon
pierced with cloves.

*

Always resist the urge to scrub,
there are other uses for a bar of soap.
Trust your own scent over those
of tuberose and heliotrope.

They're grubby little boys, each last one.
And they don't give a fig for civet, musk
or ambergris, so take care to smell
just like the girl you are.

*

And remember to wear a locket
with a little you-know-what in it.
And if you don't know what I mean
then honey, see me after class.

The Theory of Fireworks

Ephemeral is best.
Sparkle matters.

Two planes assist,
looping each other
in the sky.

       Parachuters
just distract.

Hire a pirate captain to protect
the unexploded cargo from attack.

Don't bring a cat.

Station six little fireships
to blast
      chaos
            and surprise
across the lake.

Beware the feral firefish.
Silver works.

A single artificial star should streak
and die,
      then dark
must be restored.

This most affects
the melancholic audience.

The most important law
of pyrotechnic excellence
is this:

you need to do the work of wanting
yourself,
        longing must be left
to last.

The Connoisseur

Tip: take a good sip of the chilled wine.
Don't swallow. Keep it steady
in the cup of your tongue,
but not for so long that it warms up unduly.
Smile, be a sphinx, while the other talks and drinks.
Then, at the judicious moment, lean forward
for the possibly not unexpected kiss.
When lips touch, tip the whole lot
into the opposite mouth, as it readily opens.
Most will come back, warmer, but still
with a chill edge to it, and tastily laced
with saliva. Yum! If a drip escapes,
catch it on the tip of your tongue;
lick to mop up. Best, though, if you can niftily
slip the liquid back and forth,
losing not a drop, so the gullet can claim
its modest dividend at each swap.
Snog till dry, then sit back and wait
for the next sly opportunity. As for the right wine:
a tip-top Sancerre, or Pouilly Fumé,
is what I'd recommend – though, truly,
any old white would do just fine.

Fig. II. Key Qualities in Lovers

Fig. III. Gifts for your Sweetheart

The Giveaway

When we are still strangers, glance at me once,
look away, then pin me with your eyes.

Serve me an eyebrow flash, stand straight,
part your lips.

I want you open,
I want you obvious and legible.

When we date, give me all of your attention.
Send your eyes on a voyage over my shape.

Sit opposite and mirror me.
Keep your pupils dilated at all times.

When we part, stand close and guard me
from other men. Hook your thumbs
in your belt loops.

Show me what you've got.

Advice to Members of the Uniformed Professions

No one goes doe-eyed for a notary –
you're fortunate in this, so make the most
of what fate and the State have given you.

And not just doctors, firemen, police;
out there are devotees, hungry to kiss
the pudgy fingers of optometrists,

to drag their nails through the spruce perruque
of petty sessions magistrates. Websites
exist for this sole purpose – to unite

the coat-and-button seekers with the sought.
It is your right to form a union.
But retain at least one token of your trade:

that headgear, those untethered epaulettes,
and that dog collar that just will not sit
are what have taken you this far,

so don't neglect the source of your success.
It is too soon to kick away the step, to let them
see beyond your outer shell. Who said

that they were interested in anything
beyond your outer shell? A nurse without
a nurse's clothes is much the same as anybody else.

So, public servants that you are,
you have a duty to perform your role.
Let's call it overtime. Besides, without

the stethoscope's cold tongue against her breasts,
the whistle dangling between your teeth,
how else are they to know that you are you?

Myrtus

(after Horace)

Gorgeous boy, there is no need to overdress.
I can't urge you enough – ditch the artifice.
There's no need to bring me pricey black roses.
        Thorny, unscented.

And you can lose that spider-spun suit as well.
Come to me naked – a simple myrtle sprig
bright between your teeth. Be mine, right here beneath
        this cheerful old vine.

How To Be Sexy

A girl I know did something. It is by and large just about the sexiest thing you can do.

Peek-a-boo, sideways jerk, long, slow wink, *Meetcha in the hall, honey*.

Being able to sit very still is sexy. Sphinxes knew what they were doing.

Clean hair is sexy. Lots of clean hair is sexy,

and some fellows are mildly aroused by paperclip necklaces.

Half-slips are sexy but Paula wears girdles. Girdles are not sexy.

Baggy stockings and borrowing money are not sexy.

Marlene was the absolute end in a thing and schoolgirl-scrubbed face.

The dress that makes you feel bitchy and beautiful is sexy.

Hypnotique! Intimate! Tired girls are tiring!

French perfume wafting from a pretty girl's bosom is about the nicest thing that can happen to the air!

Being seen without your makeup by somebody who always sees you in it can be sexy, provided it isn't in public.

Look into his eyes as though tomorrow's silkiest, witchiest dress is there.

Laura says a man she knows finds this look absolutely aphrodisiac. She isn't a phony.

Being delighted to be called on the phone is sexy.

It was good in your grandmother's day and it is still a powerhouse!

Enough energy to dance till dawn when other girl-blossoms are losing their petals is sexy.

Dropping your hanky, thinking all the time, being an appalling chorus girl.

Now we're coming down the home stretch on how to be sexy.

A kiss turned away, a light kiss binge, a kiss deeper than your red velvet coat.

Saying: *Do you honestly think I can sleep with every man who asks me?!*

I'd love to go into the detail about the efficacy of murmuring *Kill. Kill. Kill! Hate, hate!* while being kissed on the mouth but I'd like to get this finished, not banned.

Take your Positions

"The Arctic Chandelier" requires
A glacier, a sack of salt,
And grappling irons tipped with quartz.
The Tzar of Russia liked to sit
And watch his bravest acrobats
Attempt this cold, aerobic farce.
(In case of frostbite, bring a fur.)

"The Steve McQueen", a tricky stunt,
Involves a motorbike, a ramp,
An eloquently-spoken rant
And cushions to protect your rump.
Mid-air, your trousers need to rip
Unless you own a double onesie
(Not to try when feeling flimsy).

"The Dairy Dunker" can take place
On any farm that has a churn.
In Somerset, you'll find police
Are lenient. Lie in the corn
And set to work by clinking cans.
Remember to clean up the mess
(And give the local cheese a miss).

"The Bishop's Gambit" is a move
Imported from the world of chess.
Locate a prelate dressed in mauve
And quiz him on predestined choice,
Then dash away. He'll follow chase
And warble Latin as you run
(Get in the mood with Cote du Rhône).

Most stretching is "The Anglepoise",
Which calls out for the lightest touch:
At first you must adopt the pose
And sport a helmet with a torch.
This one is difficult to teach,
Will only function after dusk
(And someone has to be the desk).

Disruptive is "The Noisy Couch":
Encase a bed with Special K
And roll around. It may sound kitsch
But actually this one's the key
To many marriages. Look coy
And simper if the neighbours fuss
(And hoover after every sesh).

Others you might want to learn
Include the famous "Witch's Broom",
"The Legless Butterfly", "The Lean-
-ing Tower of Flesh", "The Cup of Brine",
"The Crazy World of Arthur Brown" –
Whatever works! But try to live
Briskly, blithe, and full of love.

The Lesson from the Snake

And we might take a tip from you –
split-mouth, doubler, underling –
who can at all times entertain
two propositions on the tongue, two
crooked and opposing things.

She loves me and *she loves me not*
so says the double-talking snake.
Both are real but one is not
and both are true before you speak.

Tell her every vinegar thing
you've swilled and swilled around the mouth.
Spill the lot, spit it out.
What happens then?
I couldn't say.

Don't tell. Gulp the acid down
and smile and smile and bite your tongue.
Keep it secret, keep it in.
What happens then?
I couldn't say.

Forks and forks: tangential ways
divide in two and two again, two
pairs of doubles take a turn
on what they do and never say.
And all are true before you speak
(*true and not true* says the snake).
Uncertain futures bifurcate
and every one belongs to you.

She loves me, and *she loves me not*
and both are true until you speak.
Better by far to hold your tongue
and both of them can't not be true.
Futures, futures says the snake –
in one she will belong to you.

Forget what you've been told

The kindliest fallacy
is that you should always keep things simple.
Say what's in your heart!
But romance is a craft,
the reason we sparked fire,
spat words
and searched for obscene metaphor
in dull places.

Tell me, do you want to be a lover?
Are you ever excited by shopping lists,
or the prospect of writing thank you cards
for hoards of wedding gifts?
No, because you've been told
that love is mishap and adventure,
I offer up the fundamentals:

Lesson one: you must accept
all true love is cut short –
there will never be sufficient years.
Time refuses to expand
so you must make room in your chest.

Lesson 2: Real love is painful,
a cigarette butt to the heart.
Any loss of love will burn right through you.

Lesson 3: Love does not equal happiness.
Happiness apes love,
it is a new-fangled measure of longevity.
If love always equates to happiness
I'm afraid you're still
doing it all wrong.

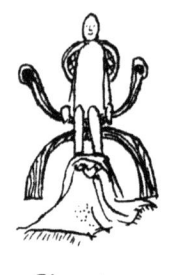
a. Shortness

b. Slenderness

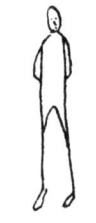
c. Bitten nails

d. Bad breath

Fig. IV. How to Disguise Deficiencies

26th May '12

Dear body,

The stitches in the skin beneath your collarbone
where you tried to rip out your heart
and eat it are tearing apart at the seams.
You are loving again, it seems.

Don't sew yourself back up
or shove your heart into hibernation,
don't starve it or fling it out in frustration.
The heart can't swim and will drown in the rain;
let it loose from its lead, before it bites again.
A hem around your hope will only fray.
So hang your heart on the washing line
and wait for the stains to fade away.

Love *your soul* x

Spring Fever Summer Cold

The first tickle is taken
for nothing,
but you know
although you don't want to.
Just a scratch in the throat.

It's like falling in love.
When it's coming
it's already there,

and there is nothing
that can be done
but to go through with it
or it goes through
with you.

Any attempt at sedating
or medicating your way out of it
is hallucinatory.

Bacilli disperse explosively.
A solid ball of ore
rolls heavily
behind your eyes,
and this misery is all
you think of.

But trust me,
on the fifth day
you are over it
and back to worrying
about the dry cleaning.
So drink plenty of fluids.

I Give You This as a Token

for Sarah Jane and Mark

In a world with too many ends, how else
but with rings can we hope to encircle and seal?
Tonight we should learn to follow this example;
what a fastening we might make of ourselves!
Let us all practise the art of continuous confluence,
like the orbitary motion of oceans that spill
into rivers returning in eddy and swirl,
the gyrating trance of the honey bee's dance.

Even now outside in the clearing sky
the arc of a rainbow looks to complete
itself in the curve of its own shadow. Not gold
so much, that it is after, as a bending to tie
one end of itself to another and make replete,
whole, without ending; to have and to hold.

Strategies for the Monogamous

If you grow bored or lose your grip, don't try
to improvise a new hold. Why take up

the plough, reshape the land you've mapped by heart,
its shifts and sighs? Remember: true bliss lies

in being known: when dirt and virtue pair
with trust, your prize is love, and love's the fruit

of work and time. The soft loam waits for your touch.
Give it your body's heat. Feel it rise.

Strategies for the Adulterous

If you are prey to moral rectitude,
this formula applies: transgression

is the medicine: ergo, purge the blood
with lies until the veins run clear. Your cure

is in the downward slide. Once free of virtue,
given to the darker side, bring on

the pulse and rise and let the games begin:
hot spill of honesty between your thighs.

How To Have An Affair

Nice girls do have affairs and don't necessarily die of them!

Suffer? Quite the contrary, one of my best friends is such a girl. (Gracious, what a greedy girl!)

It's insane to not keep your channels open, trapped by technical purity.

Lack of suitable him? Run aground on emotional reefs?

Think: Tycoon, truck driver, New York manufacturer of cosmetics.

Do not suffer at all. Admit to the sexiest of all alliances.

Once in bed it's kind of silly to fake experience.

Sunny and sweet affairs are shallow and lacking in plot.

Stick to unravelling chrysanthemums if you're not sure the love-making is first rate!

Sink into a man so completely he will never be able to unsink you…

Your body wants the agony of cliff-hanging sex and anywhere is fine as long as it's within the law.

Seduce by psychiatric consultation…

Conduct and ground rules: rump roasts (yes) wall-to-wall monogrammed towels (no).

You don't like your adorable kitty dragging a half-alive pigeon into your living room, but that's the nature of kitties.

The end of the affair? Throw beanbags against the fireplace, shred your lover's pulpy brain, fail in your brazenry.

(It's got to be better than a life stable as four-year-old peanut butter, drastically trapped by inhibitions.)

It's no talent to be a loving little stoic. Think "Tonight, boy, I'm going to get laid!"

CURES FOR LOVE

a. MINIMISE
your time with her

b. MAGNIFY
her flaws

c. ADD
more women

d. SUBTRACT
your affection

Fig. V. Four Ways to Lose your Lover

A&E

Una manus vobis vulnus opemque feret
                P. Ovidi Nasonis Remedia Amoris

You sighed and moaned and now you bleed and writhe.
This is love. This is love's other side.

They found your shining blissful yearning soul
encased in rain and dust, beside the road,

still crooning, *What a thrill to be adored!*
and pulled you from the mangled, shattered Ford.

Don't curse the gods, her, me, the lies of song
because love's flesh and metal, fire and bone.

Fractures are set, hearts mend, forget, wounds heal
and until then I'll promise that you'll feel

what you did then (A momentary sting.
A moment more. There.), flooring her, taking

those hairpin curves on the Amalfi Drive.
This is what it is to be alive.

Medicine

Go to the witchdoctor   tell him 'I was in love with you'

and he will flick out metaphors like cards   each one the punchline to the trick

more revelatory than the last   like how he says   'in your head

you were treasure hunting together   so cute in your all weather gear

your tents trowels and detectors   and hesitant analogies about the future

and you're crouching over   what looks like gold and he   beholds

himself and who he'll be   and bolts   clears the fence in one leap

clutching himself to his chest   or I guess he is a novelist

and you the model for the love interest   beautiful and difficult   you are Beatrice Lesbia

Zelda   you have a soul like a bird   there's a whole chapter on your laugh but when you read the final draft   by page three you've been

murdered or'   he continues   'you are a trapeze act   your angles of

attract and grasp   and fling and catch intuitive   and you fly across

the canvas firmament   and the hands you stretch to clasp   have skipped town

and you drop   like a shocked stomach   and break   and later when you're packaged up

in plaster in your room   he sends round some goons   to smash up

the rest of your bones   all of them   even the little ones   that's my diagnosis'

says the witchdoctor   just let the witchdoctor tell you what to do   and he will recommend

a part cure   which is to write all this down   and you have found mine here

52 Card Pickup

nec te quicquam nisi ludere oportet

Start small. One half-open eye may survey thirty
square feet of bed for several hours. Note that not one
of the seven shining hells you built is half as hot
as this field of white linen. Know all your dreams
are now the same six confidence tricks, shuffled.

Trust nobody. Not the old goon at the instruments:
the nerves splutter imperatives, but all news
is duff gen, scrambled, haywire. Be resigned,
if not accustomed, to the rank flue that opens
between heart and mouth. Learn to bluff, and bluff.

Get superstitious. Develop a taste for patterns, pairs,
but know that you're all out of luck. Here you are
sinking the black on a sure shot, snake-eyed, dropped
right in it with no getaway. You've got one bad hand
and you'll play it. Sweet nothing, and you've stuck.

Tally up. Find the same spilt deck, the same face
turning up, whichever way you look at it. Bluff,
but fool no one. There he is again, the duff joist
that brings the whole lot down. This is the house.
This is you, in bed at noon. Weeks pile up, discarded.

Elixir Amore

To make this cocktail do not scrimp, but source
the finest ingredients you can afford.
Rise early in the morning to procure them,
and carry them with care back to your home.

Lay them out by size; the afternoon
should be spent chopping, zesting, liquidising,
crushing blocks of ice to be as fine
as physics will allow, before re-freezing.

Wipe down your surfaces and scrub utensils,
hermetically seal in your fruits and rinds.

Prepare your vessel now, a pristine glass,
the kind that curves deliciously beneath
your finger and is brittle to the touch.

At evening's onset, pour the measures out
into a shaker, judging them by sight,
then shake, the motion stemming from the wrist.

This is the final opportunity
to change your mind and take a different path.
Half measures will exacerbate your case:
it's all or nothing, choose within one breath.

Once you're resolved, pour the expectant mix
into the glass, raise it up high, and toast
loves past, loves present, lovers yet to come.

Drink every drop. Repeat until you're numb.

With this ring

What a history of meaning!
How your shared past
gleams in its orbit!

And how can you bear
to wear it, now? I say,
suck it. Suck it cooking,

suck it sneezing, suck it browsing,
suck it rolling in the beds
of rebounds one and two

and slip it in the mouth of three
like Houdini got his key
and wriggle out and grab it back

and note the domestic use of rings,
in the greasy o of your bin,
the chromed hole in your sinks,

and stuff the silly thing
into a piñata and have a party
and once you've licked away the sugar

test it casually between your teeth
like in an old movie,
to see if it dents,

and believe your friend
who says *you should always
keep the gold*

and stare at it when you're
laughing, use it for fly fishing,
wear it on your big toe,

hold it up and pretend
it is the lens
in a telescope,

which rings the stars
and suggests how complete
and how in process you are.

ACKNOWLEDGMENTS

'How To Be Sexy' and 'How To Have An Affair', both by Amy Key, are assembled from words and phrases taken from Helen Gurley Brown's *Sex and the Single Girl* (Bernard Geis Associates, 1962).

ABOUT THE POETS

Jo Brandon was raised in Lincolnshire and is currently based in London. She works part-time for the Poetry Society and is former General Editor of *Cadaverine* magazine. Her pamphlet, *Phobia*, was published by Valley Press in 2012 and her writing has featured in publications including *Poetry Review, Aesthetica, Dream Catcher* and *Cake*. She can be found online at: www.jobrandon.com

John Canfield grew up in Cornwall and now lives in London. His poems have appeared in magazines and anthologies including *Oxford Poetry, Transom, Newspaper Taxis* and *Coin Opera II*. He trained as an actor, but due to a clerical error currently works in an accounts department.

Jade Cuttle is currently reading French and Russian at Homerton College, Cambridge University. She won Foyle Young Poet of the Year awards in 2010 and 2012, and second place in the 2011 Ledbury Poetry Festival Competition. She was invited to read at Ledbury Festival, and has recently performed in Parliament.

Amy Key was born in Dover and grew up in Kent and the North East. She now lives and works in London. She co-edits the online journal Poems in Which. Her pamphlet *Instead of Stars* was published by tall-lighthouse press in 2009. Her debut collection *Luxe* was published by Salt in November 2013.

Anja Konig was raised in the German language and now writes in English. Her work has appeared in magazines in the UK and the US, including *Poetry Review, Poetry London, Smiths Knoll, Magma, The Stand, Cimarron Review*, and *The Washington Square Review.*

Cheryl Moskowitz is a US born, UK based poet, translator and novelist. Her poems have been published in literary journals including *Poetry Review, Magma, Artemis* and US magazines *Drunken Boat* and *World Literature Today*. Her books include a novel, *Wyoming Trail* (Granta), poems for children, *Can It Be About Me* (Frances Lincoln) and a poetry collection *The Girl is Smiling* (Circle Time Press).

Richard O'Brien's first pamphlet, *your own devices*, appeared in 2009 on tall-lighthouse press and his second, *The Emmores*, has just been published by the Emma Press. His work has featured in *Poetry London*, the *Erotic Review*, and *The Salt Book of Younger Poets*. His blog, *The Scallop-Shell*, is dedicated to the close reading of contemporary poetry.

Andrew Wynn Owen is reading for a BA in English at Magdalen College, Oxford. He is a former winner of the Foyle Young Poets of the Year Award (2008, 2009, 2010), the Ledbury Poetry Competition (2011), The Times Stephen Spender Prize for poetry translation (2011), and The Richard Selig Prize (2013). He is currently Secretary of the Oxford University Poetry Society.

Abigail Parry worked as a toymaker for several years, and is now completing a PhD on play in contemporary poetry. Her work has appeared in *Poetry London, The Rialto, Ambit* and *Magma*, and also in various anthologies. She received an Eric Gregory Award in 2010.

Rachel Piercey was President of the Oxford University Poetry Society and won the Newdigate Prize in 2008. She is currently an editor at *Cadaverine* magazine and her illustrated pamphlet of love poems, *The Flower and the Plough*, was published by the Emma Press in January 2013.

Christopher Reid's most recent book is *Six Bad Poets*. Among his earlier publications, *A Scattering* was declared Costa Book of the Year 2009, while *The Song of Lunch* became a BBC2 film starring Alan Rickman and Emma Thompson.

Jacqueline Saphra's first pamphlet, *Rock 'n' Roll Mamma*, was published by Flarestack and her first full collection, *The Kitchen of Lovely Contraptions* (flipped eye), was developed with funding from Arts Council England and nominated for The Aldeburgh First Collection Prize. An illustrated book of prose poems is forthcoming from the Emma Press in 2014.

Liane Strauss is the author of *Leaving Eden* (Salt Publishing, 2010) and *Frankie, Alfredo*, (Donut Press, 2009), a guest poet on the Clive James website and Head of Poetry, Creative Writing, at Birkbeck College. Her poems have appeared in numerous journals and anthologies in the UK and the US.

Nicola Warwick was born in Kent and currently lives in Suffolk, where she regularly attends a poetry café in Ipswich. She has had poems in magazines and anthologies and is currently working on her first collection while undertaking a mentoring scheme with Jan Fortune of Cinnamon Press.

Ruth Wiggins lives in East London with her partner and three sons. Her work has appeared in UK magazines and anthologies, and has been commended in recent competitions. Her first pamphlet will be published later this year by the Emma Press. A book of her images of women dressed as super heroes was also published in 2008: http://amostoys.com/wwoa/index.html

The Emma Press

small press, big dreams

The Emma Press is an independent publisher dedicated to producing books which are sweet, funny and beautiful. It was founded in 2012 in Winnersh, UK, by Emma Wright and the first Emma Press book, *The Flower and the Plough* by Rachel Piercey, was published in January 2013.

Our current publishing programme includes a mixture of themed poetry anthologies and single-author pamphlets, with an ongoing engagement with the works of the Roman poet Ovid. We publish poems and books which excite us, and we are often on the lookout for new writing to feature in our latest projects.

Visit our website and sign up to the Emma Press newsletter to hear about all upcoming calls for submissions as well as our events and publications. You can also purchase our other titles and poetry-related stationery in our online shop.

http://theemmapress.com

ALSO FROM THE EMMA PRESS:

The Emmores,
by Richard O'Brien

ISBN: 978 0 9574596 4 9
Price: £5 / $9

Richard O'Brien (Foyle Young Poets of the Year Award winner, 2006 and 2007) deploys every trick in the love poet's book in this fascinating pamphlet of poems, written in response to a new long-distance relationship and loosely inspired by the Roman poet Ovid's *Amores*. An irresistible mix of tender odes, introspective sonnets, exuberant free verse and anthems of sexual persuasion.

The Flower and the Plough,
by Rachel Piercey

ISBN: 978 0 9574596 0 1
Price: £5 / $9

Rachel Piercey (Newdigate Prize, 2008) considers the dynamics of love and relationships in this stunning debut collection. Romantic but never sentimental, Piercey approaches her subject with emotional and linguistic clarity and builds up a nuanced study of passion and heartbreak, capturing everything from the extravagant surrender of early love to the raw ache and misery that can follow.

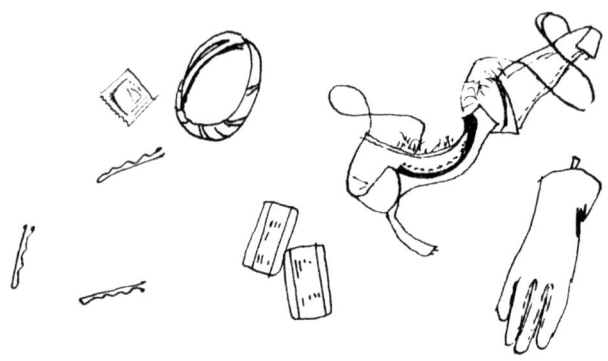

The Emma Press Anthology of Mildly Erotic Verse

ISBN: 978 0 9574596 2 5
Price: £10 / £17

A beautiful anthology which celebrates modern eroticism in all its messy, sexy glory. We see lovers imagined as heroes and hares; describing what they want in jawdropping detail (or maybe with no words at all); meeting at swimming pools, sinking into baths and magic boxes. They wonder about lost knickers, worry about caravans, and – sometimes – find themselves transformed.

Edited by Rachel Piercey and Emma Wright, with poems from Julia Bird, Mel Denham, Joy Donnell, Hugh Dunkerley, Kirsten Irving, Amy Key, Anja Konig, Ikhda Ayuning Maharsi, Julie Mullen, Richard O'Brien, Emma Reay, Kristen Roberts, Jacqueline Saphra, Lawrence Schimel, Stephen Sexton, Jon Stone, Sara-Mae Tuson, Ruth Wiggins and Jerrold Yam.

COMING SOON:

THE EMMA PRESS ANTHOLOGY OF MOTHERHOOD

Publishing 28th February 2014

An anthology which examines the depth and complexity of emotions surrounding motherhood.

THE HELD AND THE LOST, *by Kristen Roberts*

Publishing 28th February 2014

A moving collection of distinctly Australian poems about love, marriage and family life.

RASPBERRIES FOR THE FERRY, *by Andrew Wynn Owen*

Publishing 28th March 2014

Gorgeous, tart and juicy poems which are grounded in the past and bubbling with modern verve.

IKHDA, BY IKHDA, *by Ikhda Ayuning Maharsi*

Publishing 28th March 2014

A mind-blowing collection of poems about love, life, and a long-overdue introduction to the unique worldview of Ikhda Ayuning Maharsi.

THE DEAD SNAIL DIARIES, *by Jamie McGarry*

Publishing 24th April 2014

A celebration of snail culture, as told by a talented and prematurely-crushed snail poet and translated by Jamie McGarry.